No Nervous Lady

No Nervous Lady

AN INTERVAL IN THE
WIDE-RANGING LIFE OF A
SCHOOL TEACHER

BASED ON A TRUE STORY

Publisher: Jann Maree

First published in Australia 2022
This edition published 2022
Copyright © Jann Maree 2022

Cover design, typesetting: WorkingType (www.workingtype.com.au)

The right of Jann Maree to be identified as the Author of the Work has been asserted in accordance with the Copyright, Designs and Patents Act 1988.

All rights reserved. No part of this publication may be reproduced, stored in a retrieval system, or transmitted, in any form or by any means without the prior written permission of the publisher, nor be otherwise circulated in any form of binding or cover other than that in which it is published and without a similar condition being imposed on the subsequent purchaser.

Maree, Jann
No Nervous Lady
ISBN- 978-0-6455257-8-6

pp98

Acknowledgements

Writing a story about an eventful period in my life has been both a challenging and rewarding exercise.

I am very grateful to everyone who worked hard to get this story to print.

A big thank you to Euan Mitchell from OverDog Press for his editorial help and keen insights and to Luke Harris and the team at Working Type Studio for the cover, typesetting and layout.

Thank you to the Tantawangalo community and those friends who supported me during my year alone.

A special thank you to my mum Edith Callaghan whose unpublished memoir *Memories of Wild Duck* gave energy and inspiration to my story.

Thanks to my husband James for his critique of my work. From reading early drafts and advice on writing style to the shaping of the story, his support kept me focussed and on track.

And lastly, thank you to my readers for choosing to read my story.

For the women pioneers in my family

And

To the Elders past and present, custodians of country where this story took place

About the Author

Jann Maree has spent over thirty-five years as an educator. She has been a secondary college teacher in the ACT, NSW, Queensland and Victoria. She has also had stints in adult education and as a workplace trainer. Her interests include yoga, gardening and reading across all genres. She is married and lives in Central Victoria.

Contents

Tracking Back	1
The Campsite	7
The Campsite is Cleared	29
Transition	35
Alone	39
The Storm Builds	47
The Lawnmower	59
Up the Creek	65
Lost	71
Leaving It All Behind	77

Tracking Back

Jann's return to the little farm after thirty years had seemed like a good idea. Travelling to a neighbouring town to meet old friends had provided an opportunity to return again, to dig deeper into a previous story, to examine a past life.

The property now seemed remote and desolate and isolated. Long used to city living by now, the drive to the farm took far longer than she had anticipated. And yet the rough road was the only link to the community they had chosen to live in. The road had never been sealed, only patched. Weeds ravaged the roadside and the sidetracks made by meandering sheep and wombats were just the few visible signs of it ever being a thoroughfare. The forested hills were still magnificent and had maintained the striking vista that Jann and her former husband Tom were drawn to when they first drove towards the land, which, sight unseen, they had bought through an agent in the city.

The track leading to the hut had become completely

overgrown. Scanning ahead to locate the direction of the track was not possible because the tyre tracks that had given access to the hut were now lost under thistles, dry bracken and encroaching bushland. The creek that meandered through the middle of the property had to be crossed to gain access to the hut and had provided water for drinking, baking, bathing and building. When the rains came and the deluge finally happened and the river swelled suddenly and violently, the track disappeared under volumes of mud and water; it was after this tumultuous event that they were temporarily cut off from their neighbours and from using the track again for many months to come.

The creek ran parallel to the hut and divided the property in two. Crossing the creek had meant stepping across rocks that had been strategically placed to ensure a dry landing. But all that was thirty years ago now. The recent drought had taken its toll on the once pristine water course and only small pitted hollows of water remained with the carefully placed rocks displaced from their original stepping stone position.

The hut was no longer visible from the river crossing. A gentle rise in the ground in the distance was filled with tussock grass and thistles and blocked the view of the hut. Back then the grasses had provided food for the wallabies and shelter for the wombats and served to distract animals from the unfenced orchard she had established behind the hut. The orchard was long gone. Pairs of several varieties of fruit trees had been planted back then, in her enthusiasm and optimism for the success of this their new life. It had been the jewel of the garden and cultivated to provide fresh organic produce.

As she moved towards the rise, she passed a sunken ditch filled with lovegrass and rock ferns. This had been the epicentre of work for the hut. Dirt to make the rammed-earth shelter; hours of digging and shovelling dirt into a bucket, just one of the many back-breaking jobs.

The only evidence of the once thriving veggie patch was a stunted tuft of a lemon tree. It was the first fruit tree to have been planted in the garden area. Two composting bins and a clothes line had stood alongside. A fence had enclosed the entire area. There was no evidence of any of this structure now. But one very special area had survived. The still discernible location of her herb garden, formed using rocks from the creek bed, and it was still an obvious feature on the forest edge of the garden. A gratifying thing to find after so many years. This herb garden had provided not only nourishing plants and flavour for their food for two years, but tending to it had kept her grounded during the year she spent on her own.

The overgrown track now left behind; the structure of the hut came into view. The walls still stood firm — though the window frames had rotted. Weeds, huge nettles and a tangle of creeper wound around the door frame. A romanticised notion, which once had potential, was now gone. They were hardly flush with cash, but the plan had been to build a small rammed-earth hut using materials from the property, to enjoy bush living and to embrace a new community. After the hut was finished, a bigger house had been planned as a permanent dwelling and the hut was to become a studio or workshop.

For years she had wondered what had become of the hut and

how she would feel if ever she returned. There were plenty of memories of daily work schedules — either shovelling, ramming or rendering. But now the memory that lingered was a sense of abandonment. It had been a particular kind of torment to give your love to someone who you thought held the key to your future. Back then she had not yet learned that we are all the keepers of our own keys. Future, destiny, decision-making; she now knew the key is in our own hands.

The decision to move from professional jobs in the city. The decision to buy a property in the country. The decision to build a rammed-earth hut using materials from the property. All a test of a relationship, a test of physical and mental endurance. It had all ended so abruptly. She had grieved the stories she had been fed since birth. She stood awash with memories from thirty years ago. Another time. Another life. The place she had known, which had been so familiar, had all changed, changed utterly. She had changed. Society had changed. And her Australia had changed.

The land comprised forty acres and had been hived off from a larger property. It had become common practice throughout the state for farmers to sell off parcels of land in order to maintain financial stability during droughts. It was usually the poorest land on their homesteads, but could easily be sold to city slickers desiring a tree change.

A 'tree change' was the popular term for the many people who, disenchanted with the stresses of city life, were looking to seek greener pastures throughout the country. There had been attempts by the federal government to decentralise and so boost the decline of population in regional areas without much success.

Towns like Bathurst and Orange as well as Albury and Wodonga were to be amalgamated and developed as growth centres. But the growth had not been as rapid or as successful as hoped.

Even Canberra, the purpose-built national capital, was in the doldrums until the mid-1950s. Development was frustrated by bureaucratic bickering, political indifference, the Great Depression, then the Second World War. All had impeded progress. But from the late 1950s, there was a concerted effort to move government departments from Melbourne to Canberra. Rumour was rife throughout the state of Victoria that there were great opportunities to 'get ahead in life' for those prepared to relocate.

In 1968, Jann and Tom had moved from small-town Victoria to Canberra when Tom had been conscripted into the army. It suited them to move to a city with a strategy to expand to 250,000 and then to one million. No longer categorised as 'good sheep country spoiled', the town on the Limestone Plains welcomed those from interstate and overseas. Their 'first geographical' was the term later used by their marriage counsellor. They would spend eighteen years there, rear two children, and, as mature-age students, Jann and Tom would both graduate from university. As work on the great Hydro-Electric Scheme in the Snowy Mountains was winding down to completion, Canberra would see a new influx of workers. Engineers, tradesmen and skilled labourers from the Snowy Mountains Authority would breathe new life and energy into what was a public service 'company town', which had been once described by a visiting royal, prone to gaffes, as 'a city without a soul'. And with the opening of the new parliament house in 1988 they had seen their 'bush capital' transformed to a city of international renown.

And yet they had both felt that the city could no longer hold them.

At the same time there was a growing counterculture throughout the country, sparked by the protests against the Vietnam War, that gave impetus to a 'tree change' movement, which was growing organically. Many small regional towns and villages would benefit from an influx of young idealistic groups and individuals with skills that would enhance and reinvigorate the tired and depressed areas, which had long suffered from droughts and bureaucratic neglect. In northern New South Wales, Bellingen and Nimbin would be transformed dramatically. Often much to the chagrin of the original farmers and pastoralists. However, the small traders and shopkeepers reluctantly came to gradually recognise the benefits the newcomers brought with them.

Their marriage still intact, Jann and Tom had bought the property to reset their relationship, while at the same time they tried to build a new future together. Though there had been many tough times, they were young and strong and determined to investigate a different landscape and a different lifestyle. To leave professional jobs, to become landowners with high ideals and to live simply was part of their motivation to move from the city to the bush. And so, they found themselves encamped on a property at the foot of the Tantawangalo Mountain in southern New South Wales. Hereafter referred to as 'Tanta'.

The Campsite

Jann and Tom had chosen the best site for the caravan and annex. It was directly opposite the hut site on the other side of the creek. Wading through the creek with their equipment and supplies each day was a shared morning chore.

The open clearing was a perfect campsite. Nestled between slim, tall gum trees that provided shelter and shade and a level of protection, too. They built a mud-brick fireplace that housed a combustion stove with a ridiculously tall chimney that mimicked the trees surrounding them. The stove was kept alight from morning to night. How she loved that stove! It was the closest comfort she had that gave her a feeling of being at home. The kettle always on the boil and the chimney always farting smoke into the treetops as they cooked soups and casseroles and a weekly supply of bread. Its bush warmth was always the focal point when they entertained neighbours. They also erected an annex to use during the hot months to provide protection when the insects were active. But most of the time it was outdoor dining. Logs for sitting on, logs for a table and logs for burning. They had found an old metal bath at a local junk shop and had cradled it between two large tree trunks. It took ages to boil up enough water to have a bath. But unless you've bathed in a pristine creek where the water, even in summer, is still freezing cold, then a free-standing bath became an essential yet luxurious camping item.

They sat opposite each other in the cramped dining space of their newly positioned caravan home. They'd had a full day of moving dirt from the dugout to the hut site. She felt stimulated from the day. Moving around the caravan was an ordeal at the best of times — they'd stuffed as many of their essential belongings as they could into the van's small enclosures. And she thanked goodness for the annex, which had been a late decision to give them an extra room for the double bed. Tom was resourceful and had built a platform in the annex to keep them dry and well above the cold night draughts.

The toilet issue was an ongoing conversation in the bush. There's no physical button to flush away the detritus of your morning routine. And no paper to be left on the ground. They had chosen an area at the back of the hut site where an orchard was to be established. They had dug narrow, deep crevices that they straddled, relieved themselves and threw the soil on top. Exposed and in all weather conditions, this was the morning routine. But when the days were warm and still and the morning light streamed through the canopy of the forested area around them, it became a moment of contemplation where time stood still. Their future compost.

It was illegal to build a toilet too close to any creek bed and in this they understood the practicalities of keeping their water supply clean. Composting toilets were a popular topic amongst many of the environmentalists who had started a campaign protesting the logging of the nearby old-growth forest. And while Jann and Tom didn't build a composting toilet at that early stage, they constructed a very simple structure near the campsite using rough-hewn logs, and built it to resemble a bus shelter that appeared to be in the middle of nowhere. A sign was erected: 'Pit Stop'. She called it a 'deep ravine' because during its construction she had jumped into the hole with only her head above ground and enjoyed the realisation that they had just installed their first modern convenience.

They were surprised early one morning to hear the clip-clop of horse hooves nearby. She recognised the neighbour from the hill, riding his horse along the track towards their campsite. It struck her that he obviously thought nothing of trespassing. He carried a rifle on his back and from a distance looked a bit menacing. As he rode closer, she wondered whether local custom gave neighbours right of way through local property. She had a feeling he was checking out their campsite.

'Why didn't you move into the old house?' he asked.

She mumbled something about it being unsafe and that their plan was to restore it at a future date.

'Making a bloody lot of work for yourselves. Glad to see you've got a dunny, though.' A remark that made her wonder if he had witnessed their morning toilet routine.

They left the conversation hang in the air. And with those few words, off he rode towards the mountain range bordering their land. He probably thought they were a couple of city slickers who had some grandiose idea of living off the land. And in fact, if he did think that, he would have been right.

An old timber cottage that was in a state of disrepair sat on an incline and was surrounded by sparse bush and gum trees. It leaned precariously to one side and was included as part of the property deal. It had been lived in by the previous owners' land manager. The drought had reduced these once vibrant trees to spindly branches. In some parts, the soil had become a dust bowl and the remaining trees were now looked upon by the locals with respect, as if that was the only green to be seen. The rest of the property comprised a forested hilly section with old-growth gum trees, ferns and bushes. There were many rutted areas where wombats had dug their homes. The freshwater creek divided the property in two. This was the jewel in the crown, or so they thought at the time. A dislocated track weaved its way from the rusted gate at the entrance to the shallow rocky crossing at the creek bed that allowed them to drive across to the hut site.

The site for the hut was chosen and pegs placed in the ground. The foundations were earmarked and trailer loads of dirt were removed. It was hard work. Backbreaking work for him. As well, the site for the dugout trench was again earmarked. So, with shovel and wheelbarrow, it was in this trench that she started to dig. And as she dug, she was filled with a nagging feeling that nothing was going to rescue their marriage, that this whole adventure was a mirage waiting to be dispelled.

Was the end of their relationship in sight right from the start?

Three months pregnant, she had organised the wedding without fuss, but without much joy, either. She had asked the doctor after they were engaged if she could have a script for the new contraceptive pill. 'No! You're not married,' had been his curt reply. At only nineteen she had fallen in love and had opened herself totally to him, her first lover. Wasn't it every young girl's dream to marry and live blissfully together? In this she was no exception. She should have read *The Cinderella Complex*, given to her many years later. But instead, and even before they were married, she made adjustments to his straying eyes, hoping that their immature start and life together with a child would bond them.

She also realised that the stress of leaving their jobs, renting their house in the city, relocating their two children, and moving to a totally unknown place had taken its toll. They needed time. Perhaps they were seduced by the supposed freedom the lifestyle would bring. But they had also made a commitment to enter into a land purchase with fresh eyes. And so, she continued to dig.

The hut was to be made of rammed earth. They had decided making mud bricks and building with them was a very labour-intensive way to build. Formwork and rammed earth construction was their choice. The decision was made to build on the flattest part of the property. The 'flat' as they affectionately called it, or, as their neighbours reminded them, was a 100-year flood plain. 'When did it last flood?' they innocently asked their nearest neighbour, whose house was perched on the top of the highest rise in the area. According to the locals who had lived in the district for decades: 'There had been a flood a couple of years before the ten-year drought had changed the landscape.'

Reinforced in their choice of location for their hut, Jann and Tom started to plan.

It seemed strange to her now, but there was no house plan drawn. If there was a plan, it was never put on paper. Again, their neighbour on the hill reminded them, 'Constructing any building on the land was illegal unless plans were submitted to the local council and permission was then given.' The hut was to be the first stage in a building plan — 'a practice run', if you like. The intention was to build a more suitable house later as they became more skilled at rammed-earth construction. 'And we'll call it a hut for craft purposes and that way remove any obstacles that we might face from the local council inspectors and overly interested neighbours,' Tom had told her cheerfully.

Fortunately, recent rains had kept the creek that dissected the property well fed and provided them with freshwater for cooking and bathing at their campsite. But, more importantly, it allowed them to excavate an area on the flat for dirt for the nearby hut, while, at the same time, digging a ditch to allow any future floodwater to drain down the slope and into the creek.

They felt an enormous sense of achievement once the foundations had been dug and rammed. The tent they had put up nearby became their second home. She did wonder whether it would become their future residence — as she installed some mats to flatten out the grasses and soften the pitted ground, on which to place several chairs and an old table.

The foundations rammed, they rested for several days back at the campsite and made plans to improve their campsite to make it more practical. They had to settle in for the long haul.

It took some time to learn that their neighbour was affectionately nicknamed Knuckles and was a loner who had moved into a shack his grandfather had built and left to him, after Knuckles returned home from a stint of service in Vietnam. Like Tom, he too had been a conscript. But, although Tom had not served overseas, Knuckles had gone to war and he had never fully recovered from his stint in that divisive conflict. He could sometimes be heard screaming at nobody in particular, as he had what Jann and Tom thought was a meltdown outside his shack. His haunted voice echoed across the valley. Occasionally, the sounds of gunshots could also be heard. As the months went on, Jann did come to enjoy hearing him riding through their place. Yet another sound they became familiar with as they got used to bush living. But he never wanted to stop long enough for tea or for a chat. Later, when she found herself living on her own in the hut, she was glad to know that Knuckles sometimes patrolled the place. It made her feel a bit safer on her own. And perhaps he sensed that, too.

Going into town to stock up on supplies was always a major expedition. No matter how much they wanted to be independent, the reality was that they relied heavily on their weekly drive to the shops twelve kilometres along a mountain road. A long, winding, rutted dirt road took them to the nearest shop that stocked all the essentials. It also served as a café and a meeting place for the locals. When they first viewed the property prior to purchase, they delighted in the forested hills as they drove around steep and undulating corners. They felt they'd found paradise and an escape from the noise and congestion of the city. And that distance felt like an adventure back then.

Life on the land had its challenges and she had to learn to make adjustments in daily life. During their first year on the property, a federal election was called and the Hawke–Keating government was hoping to gain a third term in office. In order to vote, it was not a simple matter of dropping into a community polling booth nearby, as they had done so easily in the city. Casting their ballot required a long drive to the main town forty kilometres away.

The voting day in the federal election was no exception to her roster of daily chores. She had spent the early part of the day tidying up the caravan and topping up the gas lantern and relighting it. (It had been working erratically.) Within seconds, flames had engulfed the lantern. Sitting in the dining area of the caravan, she had grabbed the fiery thing with her bare hands and chucked it through the annex opening and out onto the ground. It exploded underneath a small, dry shrub only metres away, and the shrub was consumed in flames. She grabbed the car keys, rushed outside the caravan and into the car and drove it away from their campsite. Time seemed to stand still as she got out of the car and watched the flames cremate the shrub, a nearby tree and her gumboots. The campsite was safe for now. But her vote would not be counted in this federal election. She hoped that the Hawke government would be returned for a third term. Jann was still shaking with the realisation that she had just managed to save their home.

Tom arrived home later that day and was shocked to see the remains of the shrub outside the annex still smouldering from the fire. He had decided to drive back to the city to catch up with friends and, while there, cast his vote. Although he appeared concerned about her welfare and praised her for quick, cool-headed actions, he appeared distracted. She suspected he had other motives for going away for the weekend, but didn't want to question his actions, particularly after this other firestorm.

Too many betrayals. She ached knowing he was spending time with other women. A year before they had made the decision to leave their house in the city, he had disclosed to her that he had been spending a lot of time with a woman he had met through his job. She struggled to understand why he couldn't be faithful to her. They had looked after each other very well; they each enjoyed the other's company and produced two great children who were resourceful and happy. Their professional jobs had been secure and they'd spent the last eighteen years building their financial resources together. But once again, she was reminded of his ongoing dilemma that he felt he had done the right thing by marrying her, but had felt trapped from the start. On that occasion, she did ask him to pack up and go and be free to choose his life partner. He refused. Perhaps she was the one who was trapped. She hadn't trusted his fidelity for a long time and was always on the alert for his next affair. Her girlfriends often said that she was 'prostituting herself' by staying with him.

There's no logic to any of these decisions. Except she had invested so much into their relationship and she didn't want a repeat performance of her parent's divorce. She also wanted them to grow old together. Deep down, she knew she was avoiding facing the inevitable. How to emotionally disentangle from the man she had fallen in love with and married. She cared deeply for him.

She admired his capacity to problem-solve issues facing them, to do a lot with little, his energy and determination to ensure their lives were physically comfortable.

Jann and Tom sat quietly by the combustion stove late into that night, the warmth of the stove soothing away any thoughts of discomfort that might interrupt the energy for their busy day ahead.

The early morning routine was quickly established. The stove had been stoked before bed and, if there hadn't been too much rain or mist, it could be coaxed into flame with some paper and kindling.

A quick wash in the creek was the most challenging part of the morning: grab a towel, strip off at the creek's bank, dip. Very quickly. It could be invigorating, but more often it was just bloody cold and uncomfortable. Charge inside the annex and dress. An old metal kettle sat permanently on the stove and was always filled from the creek the night before. That first morning cup of tea was amazing. They often boiled a couple of eggs in their cast-iron saucepan, and made some toast using a long metal prong that had been craftily fashioned in order to hold it in front of the open door to the stove. A good start to the day.

The hut progressed slowly and some days it felt like they were going backwards. A heavy downpour one night completely destroyed a rammed-earth section of the construction. Building the hut one frame at a time allowed the rammed earth to set overnight. The flood plain was perfect for their building. A large expanse of flat land had been well-trodden by animals that had eaten all the grasses and tussocks. It was flanked on one side by the forest of tall gum trees that enveloped the course of the river and the length of the property. A post-and-rail fence bordered the end of the property and beyond this boundary was the 'Tanta' mountain range, where the river's water source spilled. She thought it was a majestic backdrop to their property, but an elderly neighbour had warned them to, 'Avoid trying to climb to the top. The underbrush is too dense for safe walking.'

The formwork was placed in position and filled with dirt and rammed with a long metal ramming rod. Mud bricks shaped the main entrance to the hut, as did the two front windows. The formwork was moved systematically round the base as the ramming process continued. She was intrigued with the process. As the building grew taller and more dirt was dug to fill the formwork, she could see the shape forming and it was exciting.

During this time, she had established two long garden beds and they were now eating lettuce and silverbeet. The fence around the garden bed, along with the growing hut, helped to shape the landscape around their new life. At the same time, she was back teaching and, in her free time, she continued to dig dirt from the drain, shovel it into the trailer and drive close to the hut for unloading. Which meant filling a bucket with dirt, adding sand and cement, and heaving it into the formwork. Jann and Tom were both very fit. It was during this time that she felt a renewed security in their relationship. They worked well together; they became great workmates. They laughed and cried together when a sudden rainstorm demolished a day's work. And again, when an old weather-beaten wombat decided to settle overnight in the shell of the hut.

Labouring together worked well for them, but they soon realised they had to get some outside support in order to reach beyond the windows and door frame. Once the gable ends were secured, the roof rafters could be erected. Their first serious purchase: wood from a wood yard, not cut from their bush block. The lintels were carefully chosen trunks from their land. But old window frames were found in the same junkyard where their old bath had been found.

The building grew around these frames. The apex roof with colorbond sheeting (another purchase) spanned the building. A mushroom-style canopy came low enough to shelter the verandah as well as the front and rear windows. It took a full year of hard physical work to get the hut to lock-up stage. Except in this part of the world, bush locals never locked up their houses. That was for city slickers.

It was during this time that a windstorm forced them prematurely to camp in the hut. She was grateful to have the shelter and to have re-rendered the inside walls, but there were months of internal design work ahead.

Jann had never appreciated the feelings of being in the natural environment as much as she had one day after they had reached lock-up stage. Walking behind the hut and towards the mountain range, she understood how tough life must have been for our pioneers, particularly for women. While she had the comfort of a caravan and the comfort and security of a job and town life nearby, they had managed to live quite simply using their own resourcefulness. One of her favourite books had always been the anthology of pioneer women's writing *No Place for a Nervous*

Lady: Voices from the Australian Bush, edited by Lucy Frost. Its stories and letters had a profound influence on her.

Another more personal influence had been her maternal great grandmother who had been one of the early pioneers of Central Victoria. It was said of her, that at the age of ninety, she could still drive her horse and gig into Heathcote for supplies. She wanted to explore what it meant to harness these strengths and to achieve something extraordinary. She remembered the tales her own mother had passed on to her and her brothers of growing up in the Wild Duck district, west of Bendigo. In her mother's time, there had been many soldier settlements allocated after the First World War. Jann remembered her mother saying: 'The land was quite fertile in most areas and, with the building of Lake Eppalock, the Shire of McIvor lost its most valuable land. Districts like our home at Wild Duck were submerged when the water was released in 1964 to cover the land that so many had loved and called home.'

Jann and Tom had confronted the idea of letting go of their safe and secure jobs, letting go of convenience, living with all the modern facilities at hand. Life in the city was changing. People were becoming more interested in material gains and the social fabric was disappearing. They certainly weren't pioneers, but they discovered that they could forge a life in the bush in a modern context. They had achieved some of those things simply by making the decisions they had. Whatever might happen in their future, what they had achieved so far was impressive.

The day Jann and Tom lost their caravan and annex was achingly hard. After the first year, they'd settled into an easy rhythm of daily work. Waking early was always a priority to getting a head start on the working day. However, on this particular day, the sky looked ominous so they decided to enjoy a day's rest and walk the boundary of the property. She always looked forward to these times together.

As they surveyed the land around, she felt connected to a project bigger than the both of them and to the values they shared that had first brought them to this project. They discussed their land issues and the building adventure they'd started. They really had retreated from the rest of the world. A cocoon that only they occupied. If there was to be any transformation to healing, this was their last chance. As they followed some previously walked tracks, they were aware of the still air closing in around them.

Suddenly, the air felt charged, a strong wind whipped up, trees started swaying around them, first rhythmically, then, within seconds, branches were thrashing in a blustering gale. Instinctively, they decided to head back to their campsite. But it had become virtually impossible to move. Destructive winds were now raging throughout the property. The sound of tree trunks creaking and branches snapping and falling to the ground surrounded them. The noise was deafening and very frightening. They clung to each other for support and struggled, almost crawled, against the headwinds to get back to the caravan. Dust and grit were getting into their eyes. The sky was an angry colour and she had never felt so afraid. Even though Jann felt threatened, she was aware of Tom's resilience and physical strength to ensure they stayed safe.

As they got closer to their camp, she saw that the wind had uplifted several big gum trees and landed them directly across the caravan and annex from two different directions. It was as if the caravan was the target. All they could see were their working shoes under a pile of tree trunks and branches. The annex was destroyed, the corner of the caravan crushed. There was debris all around. Fallen trees, broken branches and leaf litter had filled the campsite. The only thing that remained untouched was the bloody combustion stove and an upright from their pit-stop toilet.

They hung on to each other until the wind had calmed down. They heard later on the radio that 120-kilometre-per-hour winds had ripped through the area, causing considerable damage to surrounding property. No lives or animals were lost, but the community they had joined had a massive clean-up ahead. For days after, everything felt eerily still and quiet; even the birds could barely be heard. Jann felt they'd been tested.

They had no choice but to move into the hut prematurely. It would be months before it was finished, but it would provide shelter. A huge tree trunk had fallen directly across the creek, from one bank to the other, adjacent to the campsite. It sounds crazy, but this log became their bridge from the campsite to the hut. And it would provide them with secure access to and from the hut, as big weather patterns continued to affect their remote living zone.

The Track.

Setting up camp.

Camp site.

Author with soil for veggie garden.

Our first modern convenience (dunny)

Stage one of the build.

Roof trusses erected (author on back of truck.

Roof completed.

Destruction of camp site.

The Campsite is Cleared

Jann and Tom felt cheated of time as they slowly dismantled the ripped annex from its moorings. Part of the canvas awning was embedded in a tree trunk that had smashed their bedroom. Fortunately, the double bed was intact, but the quilt, sheets and pillows were smothered in dust and bark chips, along with their clothing. Bit by bit the awning was dismantled, bed linen and clothing removed, then bundled together ready for washing. The caravan was a disaster. The dining table that held the new gas lantern was smashed as well as the surrounding windows. Crawling in through the unhinged door allowed them to retrieve most of their supplies. On the second morning, feeling exhausted from lack of sleep and displaced from their home, they continued moving small items across the log to the hut.

Knuckles arrived unexpectedly with his draughthorse and dray to help. He would have known and perhaps was even a witness to the destruction of their campsite. Jann and Tom wondered if he was feeling a bit smug as he continued to observe a couple of city slickers living out a dream of living in the bush. Without actually offering to help or even being invited to help, he assessed the campsite and, with a slight grin, started positioning his massive horse and tacking into position, tackling the heaviest items first.

Over the rest of the day, Jann and Tom loaded their gear onto his dray, wrapped and roped it in a tarpaulin, then his huge horse pulled it back along the track towards the crossing at the creek. The water level was low enough not to cause any damage and, with some stones and small rocks strategically placed, the horse pulled their gear to the hut. Jann felt so grateful to Knuckles for his help. She knew that the words she used to thank him fell short. After Knuckles had unloaded the last of their gear, he rolled another cigarette, mounted his horse and headed off along the rutted track towards his place. A cloud of dust was all Jann and Tom could see of his leave taking.

The hut was a priority, but establishing a veggie garden was essential. Jann had always managed a veggie patch. She was thinking big. A large area was chosen in front of the hut. A fence was erected and two compost areas were built. She chose a rocky outcrop where the bush met a clearing, and established a herb garden. They also erected a clothes line within the garden area. Kangaroos and wombats were constant companions and had to be kept outside the precious garden space. A self-seeded pumpkin patch established itself outside the boundary fence and, for some unknown reason, the animals kept well away. They did have a resident red-bellied black snake that took up residence in the thickest part of the pumpkin patch. They named the snake 'Pumpkin', and their two Persian cats would sit for hours and stare at Pumpkin as it moved throughout the vines.

After time-out from earning an income, it was time to find another job. Jann was an experienced secondary school teacher who had taught for eight years in the city. Their cash reserves were running low and it was her decision to apply for an English-teaching position at a school 70 kilometres away. They needed more funds to buy solar panels, batteries and a refrigerator. She didn't give much thought to the long drive; it was what some of the locals did just to secure employment.

Jann got the job and faced the reality of the drive. She did a practice drive to the school and chose a short cut on a dirt road that logging trucks used. In hindsight, this was not a clear-headed decision. The logging industry was active in their district, as were the conservationists trying to stop it. The road was narrow with lots of gullies and bridges that slowed the journey. The trucks were hazardous.

Her year at this school had its challenges. It may have given them financial respite for the short term, but, at the end of her contract, Jann was depleted from the constant drive as well as the energy needed to engage and motivate the teenagers. During the weekend and especially during the school holidays, she continued to maintain the veggie patch and assist with the building of the hut.

One of Jann's jobs was to help render the inside walls of the hut. The decision was made to use fresh cow manure. Fortunately, one of their neighbours had a herd of cows and he was almost eager for them to collect as much manure as was needed for the render. Except the manure was not to be scraped off the ground. It had to be hot and fresh.

So, carrying a wide-rimmed shovel with a long handle, Jann crept up behind a cow and waited. They shat so often that she didn't really have to wait too long. The poo splattered onto the shovel with a weighty expulsion forcing the shovel to the ground. The sloppy poo was quickly put into a bucket, then sand and milk powder were added, and their render mixture was ready.

Their nearest neighbour offered to assist with bagging the render onto the internal walls. This process had to be done quickly to avoid hard lumps in the surface. Bagging to a smooth finish was needed. All went well until two days after the render had been applied, when there was a foul sour smell in the hut and worms were crawling through the drying surface. They had to resurface the walls with a proper sealant. So much for cutting corners and using milk powder to lighten the colour of the walls.

Cupboards for the kitchen were built, and an old wood-fire stove and chimney were installed. Solar panels and batteries were connected to provide electricity for lighting, the refrigerator and partially power a hot water system. Bathing in the creek was no longer an option, so a small additional room was built off the hut to fit a square bathtub, complete with a plumbed tap connected to an external tank. Their hot water system was never able to heat water above warm. It was adequate, but Jann often longed for a hot shower.

The morning routine had changed from the campsite. They now had an in-built stove always full of burning embers. She had also purchased a gas stove top for back-up. It felt like they were cheating, but after a year of roughing it, it felt luxurious. Instant hot water for a morning cup of tea. The toilet remained the dug-out pit alongside either a lemon, pear, cherry or peach tree. The orchard was thoroughly nourished.

Jann couldn't say the same for her experience of squatting over a dirt pit each morning, particularly when it was raining or when she had her period. On these occasions, it took some real effort to manoeuvre an umbrella in one hand and toilet paper in the other. She remembered wryly the stories of the pioneer women and their striving to maintain some semblance of 'gentility' *Stuff gentility,* she thought. *What about dignity?*

It's definitely no place for a nervous lady.

Transition

After two years of bush living, Jann and Tom's decision to leave the city and the effort needed to rebuild their lives had taken its toll. The remoteness, the extreme weather conditions, and the bush-living challenges could easily be blamed for their decision to separate. However, looking back now, it became clear to Jann that Tom was not committed to sustaining their marriage, but had chosen to use the tree change as an opportunity to be free. She accepted that he had no idea how this move would resolve, except that his investment in exploring other relationships was one of the drivers to end their marriage.

Tom's decision to abandon the property and to leave her didn't come as a shock to Jann. For several months leading up to this decision, he had become more and more distant. His absences from the property increased. The harder she hung on emotionally, the harder he pulled away. That seemed to be the pattern. She could see what was happening, but she was unable to do anything to alter its course.

They were well aligned as a couple, rearing two children and supporting each other as they studied for their degrees and developed their careers. They had succeeded in growing together as a young family, so it seemed incomprehensible to her that their unit would not survive. However, they were no longer going to be a couple.

The week before Tom announced his intention to leave, Jann had been weeding the herb garden. She remembered it was mid-morning and she had just managed to arrange the rocks to support the length of herb garden. It had been such a hard project to collect the rocks from the nearby riverbed. It had been even more challenging to shovel rough soil from underneath the nearby gum trees into a bucket. It's a wonder she hadn't stumbled over fallen branches and twigs just to get to the riverbed and back again while carrying either a rock or a bucket of soil. No project had been easy for her and creating this garden was no exception. But the sun had felt warm on her face then. She looked up when she heard his vehicle start up. Tom had not acknowledged her, nor waved as he started to drive away and his eyes stared ahead. And in that instant, she lost all strength in her legs and stumbled, as though she was being pulled to the ground. She knew then that he was leaving. The herb garden faded in front of her as she looked up and watched his utility disappear down the track towards the creek.

Tom's return later that day was to organise a vehicle swap so he could attend a conference in the city. He was not travelling alone. He was travelling to the conference with his new lover.

Jann remembered it was the Monday afternoon of a long weekend. She had stood looking through the window from inside the hut. She watched the car approach along the tyre tracks worn down from so many trips across the paddock. Trips to the village to get supplies. Trips to her teaching jobs. Trips in the utility loaded down with dirt for the mud-walled hut. The move to the property two years before was a decision she had agonised over. It had meant resigning from the security of her teaching job. But it did feel like a fresh start, a new way forward together. Tom, of course, had other ideas — or so he had told her later.

Obviously, Jann knew then that this wasn't his usual homecoming. He had been away so often these days. The car seemed to falter as it reached the hut — or was that her anxiety to stall the finality of their parting? And as she tried to bring their shared history into focus, to feel a sense of certainty in her life, she could not. Looking through the double doors of the mud-walled hut, the car — *her* car now — came to a stop. In that brief moment, she felt alone in her life and in her marriage.

Jann opened the door to Tom and they embraced briefly and pulled apart. He had returned from a weekend away; a course in Sydney he had said. Quietly, seeming to hold his breath, he told her that he was leaving, that he had spent the weekend with his new lover.

Jann had rehearsed her part in this conversation so many times. In fact, she had been rehearsing living without him for the last few months of their marriage. No more hanging on. No more making emotional adjustments. No more pretending his affairs weren't happening. She no longer had a script to follow. The long weekend she had spent alone had forced her to acknowledge that their twenty-year marriage was over. She had felt crippled with him and crippled without him. More than anything, a sense of dread and confusion engulfed her.

Alone

In those first few hours, everything visible around Jann seemed the same. She stared, almost mesmerised, at the dirt track leading away from the hut. *Well, I suppose this is it,* she thought. Stuck in the middle of nowhere, kilometres from the nearest town, living in an unfinished dirt hut with few comforts and the responsibility of a ridiculously large vegetable garden to manage. And very little wood chopped for the stove.

She started to laugh, or perhaps it was an utterance she had yet to give meaning to. She didn't feel anything really. 'How strange,' she said out loud. She had been rehearsing his leave-taking for years and grieving his potential absence while still together. What a distorted reality and a potential loss of connection to him.

Jann realised she had to finish the day's jobs before preparing for the week ahead. She slowly opened one of the glass doors to go outside to check on some of the recently planted veggies and to wind up the long hose. She stood halfway between the hut and the outside earth floor. The overhanging roof was finished, but the raised wooden floor was yet to be laid. She mused, 'I don't even have an enclosed patio area to sit and enjoy the view.'

The vegetable garden was well established with long rows of cultivated soil, well protected by straw and enough vegetables to feed the entire neighbourhood. The sun was low in the sky and threw a protective glow through the leaves of the grapevines as she mechanically walked into the garden and checked the young seedlings and wound up the hose. She picked some lettuce leaves to make a salad for her dinner, then decided against the idea and threw them onto the compost bin as she walked past. 'WHAT A BASTARD!' she yelled.

Her first morning alone. The wood stove yet to be lit. Jann had forgotten to add a few logs before going to bed to keep the embers going. And she had run out of gas for the mini stove. She told herself that the morning cup of tea would have to wait.

Outside for the morning dash to the pits to relieve herself. 'And I don't even have a bloody proper toilet,' she muttered. She suddenly felt very alone, isolated and abandoned.

Jann remembered that first day alone vividly. Why? Because she felt physically so strange. It was as if some part of her body was missing; a hollowness, a peculiar feeling of dread. She kept taking long, slow breaths, but it made her feel lightheaded and her stomach felt heavy. She was now on her own and a deep sense of loss and grief tightened its grip on her.

She spent most of the day inside the hut. She remembered looking around the rectangular room as if to take it all in for the very first time. A mezzanine floor suspended over the kitchen area held their books and her teaching resources. There was extra space for a couple of beanbags. An effort to create a relaxed and separate space for reading. A handcrafted wooden ladder was moved from this end to the other end of the hut where a mezzanine floor was built as a storage area with a single bed, cupboard and extra storage space — an escape route designed to protect against any 100-year flood. And the flood did come.

Their old hutch held her precious crockery and an old wooden pantry cupboard contained stored food. The double bed (handbuilt) fitted in the corner of the room and an old weathered couch sat at the foot of the bed. A comfort she couldn't do without. Nor could she do without her macramé creations suspended from the roof with healthy potted plants cascading into the roof space.

Jann had always loved potted plants. A few of her favourite plants came with them and were positioned strategically around the campsite. It seems quite absurd now when she thinks about dragging the damn things so far. They were awkward to pack, awkward to transport, but, ironically, they gave the campsite a homely touch. Which is quite ridiculous, in that they were surrounded by a forest of trees and plants. Such is the lure of familiarity and the connections they provide to keep us feeling secure and grounded. Now they were safe on the inside, she felt better about having brought them all.

Her cherished dressing table, adorned with a few pieces of jewellery, was positioned next to the bed head. The kitchen comprised a bench with open cupboards underneath. A sink and a tap attached to the outside tank. Their Queen Anne table stood jammed against the two large windows. A small area off the room was the bathroom, with a square bathtub and a shower recess above.

Together, they had decided to build this hut. Alone, Jann had decided to furnish it this way. Attractive, homely, with a vase of flowers always on the window ledge. She had found an attractive Vermeer print while fossicking in a junk shop, which she hung on the mud wall next to the dresser. The print was of a young woman pouring a beaker of milk from a ceramic jug into a bowl on a wooden table, to one side a cane basket held chunks of bread. *That's me,* she had thought. A woman alone in a rammed-earth hut, in a primitive environment, in a faded picture.

After a while, unable to settle, Jann packed a few things to eat and went down to the river. A place where she always found solace. She was trying to get away from the feeling of not being good enough, of blaming herself for Tom's decision to leave. Her muscles felt tense. She remembered that it was her story, too, as much as it was his. It was time to get immersed in work and to regain some sense of balance in her life. And so began her story of living alone on the property in the hut they had built together and her gradual recovery from the pain of separation into a full life on her own.

That first week. Nothing could have prepared her for the loss she felt. Their children had left home. This loss was a rite of passage accepted as children leave home to live independently. She accepted this time as one of celebration — everything parents prepare their children for. Independent thinkers, a maturing curiosity about the world they're about to venture into, without the eyes of a parent always keeping checks on them. She remembers how ironic it was that she was now without any family around her. Everything in her world up until then had been achieved through the lens of family. Her lens felt myopic.

She remembered driving into the village to stock up on supplies, and on her return a pile of recently chopped wood had been neatly stacked and placed near the door. She can vividly remember driving into the nearest town some forty kilometres away and being sideswiped by a truck turning left in front of her. Had she become invisible? Her car's entire right front fender was crushed. She can remember driving her battered car into town again the next day and seeing Tom standing on the side of the road, hitching a ride into town because his utility had broken down. *Collective karma,* she thought, as she drove away from him after he had waved her on, as if she was just another passing motorist. Dismissed.

She also remembered sitting in the hut late into the night preparing notes for her first adult TAFE class. Her teaching life.

If anything kept her grounded during this time it was her professional world. She had just won an adult education position as a literacy leader at the local TAFE college. Interviewed some weeks previously, she had been told by letter that she had secured the position well ahead of other applicants. Her timetable included supporting vocational students' literacy in classes that included Mechanics, Horticulture and Cooking.

It turned out that the Cooking class provided her with a three-course meal once a week. How she loved that class — not because the students she supported were particularly welcoming or easy to work with, but it was because she got to eat a substantial meal each session. And this aspect of her life turned out to be one of the life rafts thrown her way. The only downside to this full-stomach arrangement was the class finished late at night, which meant a long drive home. And a dark welcome to her log-crossing over the creek to the hut.

She had also been timetabled to deliver an Outreach Program funded by TAFE to teach church volunteers communication skills. A ten-week program supporting conscientious adults who were keen to continue their religious life in service of their community. Another life raft was to appear through one of the female volunteers who became a very dear friend during this time.

She remembered how much couples take for granted as they organise their days around each other. She no longer had access to the utility or the use of the trailer to collect wood, to transfer soil to the vegetable garden, to collect straw from the hardware store, or to take it in turns to do the shopping and the cooking or checking on the children.

The days settled into a rhythm. She worked physically hard in order to stay focused. Her new teaching job required a great deal of preparation. A folder of structured notes was written to support each week's lesson. Keeping the volunteers' course engaging was the key to a successful outcome for them. Many were under-confident and new to the volunteering role. The agenda from the start was to set a program and to establish clear guidelines that were negotiated by the group. She remembered thinking how vulnerable she was during those weeks. At the same time, this particular program had given her a solid structure and had reinforced her capacity to communicate clearly. As she drove home from each weekly session, she always felt exhausted from covering up her emotional distress and at the same time planning her next session for the following week.

Her Cooking class required her to support vocational students to follow instructions, to read and follow recipes, and to learn how to prepare and serve food. Returning to the property after class finished became hard. Not only because she returned to an empty hut, but because she had to drive twenty-eight kilometres in the dark to the village and then another twelve kilometres along the winding dirt road to the property. Once at the main gate, she had to stop the car, keeping the headlights on the latch, open the gate, drive the car through, stop the car, get out again and close the gate. Then drive a few metres and stop at the next gate… Once she arrived at her parking spot on the side of the creek opposite the hut, she had to 'walk the plank', as she would later joke to friends.

The Storm Builds

After many months of living alone in the hut, Jann had started to feel normal again. She had started her early morning routine of doing a few yoga stretches before breakfast. Her aloneness and anguish was slowly dissolving into the background, as she developed more energy for thinking about other things. She had always been highly organised, even precise about her physical wellbeing, which included eating really well. She practised yoga regularly and had attended many classes throughout the years of her marriage. And she believed this practice, along with eating fresh from the garden, had kept her physically fit and grounded and enabled her to complete her teaching degree, while, at the same time, raising and caring for two children.

The early morning light entered the kitchen window and was her personal alarm for getting up. The vegetable garden came into view as a morning cup of strong leaf tea brewed in her old pottery teapot. Time in the orchard, with time to reflect on the day's weather, and a check on the battery-operated solar system. How luxurious it was to have an excess of energy supply, especially with a recently installed refrigerator. Yoga practice on the mat next to the bed, a lukewarm shower and ready for breakfast.

There was laughter in the hut again. She had not expected that. Returning from work the previous night, Jann had to walk the plank carrying her books and shopping as usual, but unexpectedly she had stopped midway across the log. For the first time, she realised how normal her unusual living situation had become. The log-crossing had almost become effortless; she no longer had any concern about falling in, as she had done on a couple of occasions, or dropping her precious resources into the water below. She felt less guarded and she felt she was becoming a different person. The car lights beamed brightly across her path and created a narrow-tunnelled opening through the forest and dimmed slightly towards the path that led to the hut. She looked around her. This place she thought was unique. The stillness. The light through the trees. She felt cocooned by both.

As Jann walked closer to the hut, she became aware of a movement nearby. Previously, the movement would have alerted her to a potential threat. But now she remembered it was the old wombat stretched across her walking path, making scraping sounds as it made a dugout in the dirt for the night. The wombat had decided to spend the night a few metres from the hut's entrance. Not wanting to drop her bags in front of the animal, or walk back across the log in the semi-darkness to get her torch, she cautiously side-stepped the flea-bitten animal and shuffled towards the hut doors.

She couldn't tell whether it was a sense of relief or a sense of adventure that made her laugh when she opened the hut's doors. Pulling the suspended cord to switch on a light, she felt confident as she dumped her bags, grabbed her spare torch, then returned to the car, turned off the headlights and ignition, then walked the plank once more through torch light to her hut home.

The day of the flood started like most days. It was a Saturday and Jann had the weekend free to catch up on her garden chores, do some hand-washing and catch up on some quiet reading. There was a stillness in the air that felt alarmingly similar to the day the windstorm had destroyed their campsite and forced them to move prematurely into the unfinished hut. She checked the garden for produce and noticed with a sense of satisfaction how her herb garden was producing an abundance of salad herbs.

Looking skyward, her attention was drawn to the clouds once more. They had changed colour and shape since her early morning check. In the short time she was in the garden area, they had formed into low dark sheets of deep, murky grey. *There were to be no cottonwool clouds today,* she thought, *and probably no outdoor work can be done, either.* She had chosen not to listen to the news and the weather forecast on her car radio on her return from work the previous night. Something she always did; as each farmer did. No mobile phones back then.

A familiar sound of horse hooves drew her attention as she was about to turn on the car radio. Knuckles on horseback. Jann assumed he was on his usual trek through her land and her space. 'Are you storm-ready?' he yelled from a distance. His voice was muffled from under his weather-beaten hat. 'You're a sitting duck on that flood plain, you know.' A loud boom above echoed his harsh words.

'I can look after myself, but thanks very much for your concern.'

'No region is safe from flooding,' he replied. 'And that includes your place. So get yourself organised, because a storm front is going to hit us in a couple of hours' time and it could sweep you away in seconds.' With that warning, he turned his horse around and disappeared into the distance towards his place.

Irritated at his intrusion and his aggressive tone, Jann slammed the car door shut and turned on the radio. And yes, heavy rain and hail was forecast for the district. Not just heavy rain, but with the warning of potential floods, too.

Back in the hut, she started to think about Knuckles' advice. *Get myself storm-ready, he said.* Visibility had become impaired as she looked through the window and started to feel anxious about living in an isolated hut some distance from her nearest neighbour. She remembered only too well the windstorm that had destroyed their campsite. Back then, she was not alone. She had a mate who would protect her. She suddenly felt very vulnerable.

In less than an hour, strong rain began to fall. The land in front of the hut, normally dry, was now steadily becoming saturated with water. The vegetable garden, a sunken dish, was filling with water. The realisation that she was cut off only occurred to her when she heard a loud boom as the river broke its banks and moved across the flood plain in front of the hut.

'Stay calm,' she told herself, as she started to gather together some food, small items of furniture, crockery, some clothing and her precious teapot, then climbed the ladder to the mezzanine floor where she started stacking her things. A wave of grief hit her as she watched the flood waters engulf the vegetable garden and form a lake of water across the front of the hut. She wrapped herself in a doona cover and watched the rain pelt furiously against the windows and glass doors.

The power of the floodwater was extraordinary. The landscape changed in a flash and she could no longer identify the area immediately outside her home. Debris from the riverbank had found its way close to her front door. All her efforts mowing the front paddock of grass seemed so futile, so ridiculous now. Knuckles had been right. Everything could have been lost in an instant.

Jann slept fitfully through the long night. Woken frequently and on high alert. She remembered the feeling of intense relief when, in the morning, the rain had eased and, along with this hiatus, a stillness had descended and she felt safe enough to open the hut door.

She would never forget what she saw that morning. Her property looked like a junkyard. Debris of all descriptions had emptied into the vegetable garden. The garden beds had been flattened like a pancake. And the vegetables had been shredded and flattened. The only remaining semblance of her work was the rockery that housed the herb garden. No herbs were visible, only the border of rocks. The orchard survived, but could not be used as a toilet in the short term. Her current pit was filled with water. What a disaster!

Jann thought she heard a loud voice from the other side of the embankment over the roar of the water. 'Stay indoors. Avoid leaving the hut. Don't try and cross the river, it will sweep you away. The water may be deeper than it appears.' It was Tom. Relief swept over her. No longer alone.

He couldn't be seen through the bush, but she was able to let him know that she was okay and had plenty of food for a couple of days. She saw a brief glimpse of his utility moving slowly away from the other side of the flood plain.

The day ahead was hard. She was distressed by the mess of her surroundings and the loss of her vegetables. Her pioneering spirit had gone. Her marriage had gone. And the hard work she had put in since living alone was almost gone, too.

The next morning, the flood had receded enough for her to walk outside. The paddock was littered with debris and the water had receded, leaving a trail of twig-and-leaf mulch strewn everywhere. The vegetable garden was exposed; it was a mess. But a mess that could be rebuilt. That's what the pioneers would have done.

She walked the length of the paddock to check on the river crossing they had used to drive the cars across when they had first arrived. The water surge was extraordinary. A tree trunk had been carried from upstream and lodged itself between several large rocks. Perhaps she could use this tree trunk to support her crossing to the other side.

'Don't even think about it,' a voice yelled at her, from across the rapidly moving surge of water. It was Knuckles on horseback.

'You won't be able to cross for several more days. It's too friggin' dangerous.'

Jann was jolted by the strength of his words and remembered

bursting into tears. She yelled back, 'I can't do this anymore. It's too hard. Everything about this place is just too hard. Too many setbacks.'

'You're doing okay. It takes guts to live here on your own. I watched the storm from my place and I knew you'd be safe if you stayed inside the hut.'

She raised her arm in a gesture to Knuckles by way of thanks and headed back through the quagmire towards the hut.

Exhausted from lack of sleep, Jann lost all focus on the landscape around her and made the decision to leave the property before she even stepped back into the hut. She had already worked hard to let go of the married life she had planned; now it was time to let go of her plan to live in a rammed-earth hut on a flood plain in the middle of nowhere.

Author forming border for vegetable garden.

Author tending the thriving vegetable garden.

Compost bins and herb garden.

Looking through vegetable garden at finished hut.

Front porch

Mezzanine library.

Jann relaxing by the Tantawangalo Creek.

Conservation Protest.

The Lawnmower

Jann's mind wandered. Pools of memories flooded her head. She remembered how she was determined to mow the grass around the hut. The old Victa mower had seen better days. Jann and Tom had bought it secondhand and it had served the family well, keeping their suburban grass neat and tidy. Without a catcher and with a dirty, frayed starter rope, they had still got good use from it. She enjoyed the sound and the rhythm of mowing. The finished area always looked neat and tidy. *A feeling of being in charge,* she thought. Now perhaps that had become her therapy.

They had been mates for twenty years, she and the old mower. Together they had left a legacy of many neatly mown lawns. Together they had pushed and dragged, and together they had worked hard. She remembered the sense of pride that had fuelled her decision to mow the paddock in front of the hut. She hoped her neighbours wouldn't hear the shredding noise of her mower as it sheared clumps of weeds and bark. Their animals usually took care of the grass. Thistles. Couch. Paterson's Curse. The mower spluttered in response as it always did; she had to pull the rope a second time. As she surveyed the area around the hut, she reflected on the two years as city slickers they had worked this land together.

Twelve months of hard labour, ramming dirt and making bricks yet still no verandah or toilet. It was amazing how readily they had learnt to do without. Weeks of digging, shovelling and ramming had not brought them emotionally any closer. Their plans to get back to nature, to leave the city and to rescue the marriage. Jann had wanted to believe it all. She had interpreted the move to the land as an opportunity to rebuild. She had wanted to believe in it all. For years their relationship had been suffocating. She had watched when other women were around. Others had noticed, too. How she had hated that. 'He's always on the make,' her friend Angie had observed, one night at a party. And she had always felt threatened and insecure. Waiting for the next time.

The orchard at the back of the hut had always been the most difficult to mow. She had planted the orchard in pairs. Two of every fruit-bearing variety she knew. Her favourite was always the cherry. The trees stood so firmly rooted in the soil, their maturing trunks leaning towards each other. She mowed around each trunk with as much care as she could manage. They would remain partners, as she had planted them. They would still be together after she left.

Jann and Tom had planted grapevines around the outside of the vegetable garden fence, then surrounded them with protective wire netting. They were growing well. 'Next year the vines will give fruit,' she mused, as she manoeuvred the mower nearby. She doubted she would still be there to enjoy them.

The vegetable garden still remained her constant and gave structure to her day when she wasn't teaching. It had to be looked after on a daily basis. The straw mulch they had used to protect the many young seedlings they had planted together had rescued her now thriving plants.

'Did you close the veggie garden gate?' Jann and Tom shared the responsibility of keeping the garden gate shut to protect the plants from being trodden and eaten. The old wombat, wallabies and, not forgetting, the neighbour's cattle had to be kept out. Except for Pumpkin, the red-bellied black snake that had taken up residence both in the pumpkin patch and in one of the compost bins. Its tail was always poking out as it slithered through the layers of vegetable and straw matter. The two lemon trees were the first fruit trees to be planted in the vegetable garden. They still remained. Thirty years later.

Jann moved the mower further away from the hut. She looked back and saw the hut, her home, through different eyes. It really was only temporary, perhaps even a fantasy, this notion they had a principled lifestyle in tune with nature. It no longer felt like a rational decision to leave behind a significant teaching position that ensured a substantial salary and career future to live on an isolated parcel of bush land in the middle of nowhere.

She thought about the friends she had left behind and the new ones she had made during this time on her own. Both had supported her in her grief during the early days of the separation, and both had given her a comforting place to stay whenever she needed. They had also encouraged her to keep participating in the local forest campaign. Logging in old-growth forests was an ongoing divisive issue, and the campaign gave a voice to the local residents who were deeply concerned about the land around them being systematically destroyed and the quality of their water. As a newcomer to the district, Jann remained hesitant in part because her husband and his recent girlfriend were active members of the protest group. But she also had reservations because she had met some of the forestry workers whose teenage children she was teaching.

Distracted, the mower moved across a rock and spliced it in two, one piece narrowly missing her near-naked feet. In her reminiscing, she had not seen the danger. The engine became sluggish and hesitant. 'Just keep going for a while longer,' she coaxed. With each turn, she clung more tightly to the handle. Anxious to finish the mowing, she accelerated far too eagerly and the mower stopped. A wailing sound echoed around her. All these years of frustration and humiliation. Her acceptance of it all. Something exploded within her.

It may have been minutes before Jann realised that the wailing sound had come from her. She sat close to the mower and felt a strange comfort in its heat. A stillness cradled them both. She grabbed the spark plug and burnt her fingertips. She looked at her pink, swelling fingers. *So, you've been burnt,* she thought. *Keep your cool.* It was just a temporary setback.

She tugged at the cord and the mower burst into spasms of sound, hardly smooth and rhythmical, but ready for action again.

The paddock in front of the hut still had to be mowed. And then she could move on. *Greener pastures,* she thought wryly. She gripped the handle with new determination.

Up the Creek

The creek was the drawcard for purchasing the property. And while the mixed species of eucalypts grew in clumps over the entire landscape, the gums bordering the entire length of the creek were magnificent. Tall and erect, each tree was imposing and had a soft canopy from which leaves fell to provide a carpet-like footing as Jann and Tom walked along the creek-bank trail to inspect their new place in the bush.

The deal settled, the farmer spent several hours walking the length and breadth of the property with them. He talked about the importance of the creek to the locals and how it was crucial to maintain and respect the stream's vital flow and water purity. 'This water is our lifeblood. Without it, neither we nor our cattle would be able to work this land. That state-forest mountain range you can see beyond this place is the source of our pristine water supply.'

Back then, the stream flow was strong and had many powerful

currents over its rocky path. Apart from the land's remoteness, it was the creek's cascading waters that pulled them in.

During their time together, Jann and Tom had never explored the entire length of the creek. Too busy building. So, Jann invited her new friend Kat from the Volunteer Course she was running to walk upstream with her until they reached a section of the creek the locals often talked about. It was a place where enormous boulders blocked the creek's path and water cascaded over huge rocks, forming a gully deep enough to swim in. She had heard that it was about a kilometre upstream.

'You've lost a lot of weight. Have you been eating properly?' Kat asked, as Jann greeted her on the morning of their planned walk. They hadn't seen each other since her friend had found her sitting on a kerbside. A truck turning left had crushed the front fender and bonnet of her car. Jann had been badly shaken and was relieved to be comforted by Kat as she took charge, rang the police and, after some interrogation by the local officer, took Jann to her place.

In answer to Kat's concerned look, as she continued to scan Jann from top to toe: yes, she had lost a lot of weight in those early months. What Jann had chosen to keep to herself was a decision she made at the outset to eat well. A sort of keep-me-on-track plan. An old battered recipe book that had been used to feed the family for years was resurrected. A dish from each section chosen for most nights of the week. It wasn't hard with the vegetable garden as the main source of fresh seasonal greens, along with nourishing herbs from the garden. Obsessed with food choice, her two children were fed on a vegetarian diet for years until the eldest came home from school one day and put a two-litre bottle of Coca-Cola in the refrigerator and started frying a lump of red meat on the freshly cleaned stove top. *Yet another reminder to let go,* she thought.

Bathers on, picnic lunch in their backpacks, Jann and Kat set off. Neither of them had walked upstream before. Jann warned her it would involve some rock-hopping where rocks clumped together. 'The rocks can be slippery, too.' The water was ankle deep in some sections and made walking on the sandy bed quite easy. In other parts the rocks were like stepping stones and seemed to be strategically placed. She drew Kat's attention to the clearing where the original campsite was located.

'How did you cope roughing it for so long?' Kat asked, staring at the cleared and flattened grassy area. 'It's one thing to have a camping holiday, it's entirely different to set up a long-term living space in a caravan in the bush without any proper modern facilities.'

Any answer Jann gave would have sounded insubstantial, so her response was to acknowledge that once they had made the decision to leave their jobs and live in a rural community, that decision would be supported by the conditions the bush demanded of them. 'Once the first step is made, the rest propels you forward.' Jann quoted Goethe: 'Until one is committed, there is always hesitancy, the chance to draw back, always ineffectiveness.'

Kat smiled. 'Typical literacy teacher,' she said.

Before moving past the area of the campsite, Jann pointed out a large rock partially submerged and nestled neatly against the log bridge. 'That rock was my soap holder for a short time. It was my bathroom until a neighbour found the single bar of soap and removed it.' A reminder that seclusion doesn't give permission to pollute the crystal-clear waters. And privacy comes at a price in a rural community. 'The rock also served as a platform for tickling and grabbing the rainbow trout,' she boasted.

Further along the creek, a huge boulder with a flat surface had been Jann's favourite sunbaking rock. Naked, of course. So many memories of a peaceful and sometimes sexy time together. This intimate memory was not shared as they continued wading upstream.

The water was as clear as glass. They stopped often, sat on the sediment-rich bank and removed their shoes in order to sink their toes into the sand. Taking a moment to check their surrounds, it was obvious Jann had been living in a secluded paradise. Pure mountain water against the banks of wild and rugged eucalypts. Ferns were abundant, too. Kat asked Jann why she stayed in her marriage for so long when it was obvious it was not working.

Jann replied, 'I learnt to go along and make things work. I didn't want to look too closely at the uncomfortable truths in our life together. I ignored what didn't fit into our story; that we were doing okay. I fell in love with Tom and that love was like an electric charge for me. What was missing was the connection wasn't secured.'

'But you still like men?' Kat asked.

'Mostly. Especially for one thing, I suppose,' Jann answered.

'Me too,' Kat grinned in reply.

Eventually, Jann and Kat arrived at their planned stop. The

locals were so right. In front of them, the creek was transformed into a rocky gorge with a cascading waterfall creating an idyllic swimming hole. Behind the swimming hole was a boulder that took up the entire creek bed and was a dead-end to their creek walk.

'What a tranquil bush setting,' Kat whispered, as she undressed to her bathers and gingerly waded into the cool water.

Jann added, 'The locals often talked about this creek as a reprieve from hot temperatures that often hit this area in the peak of summer. Their children had a smooth rock formation to climb and slide into the water hole. But only when the water current flowed strongly enough.'

Jann noticed a walking track that meandered close to the creek's edge, just visible alongside the swimming hole. 'The story goes that this area was important to Indigenous families who depended on a freshwater source. I'm told by the locals that the tracks were the basis for their songlines and gave them a grid reference to this district. It's not easy to spot the trails, but the locals who know the area well point to evidence that tracks do thread along the creek bank throughout this entire region,' she explained.

Lost

Jann and Kat decided to climb the embankment to check out the track above the boulder. And to find the creek on the other side of the massive rock formation. Scrambling up the side by using ferns as levers, they reached an area of compacted dirt. They realised the track was a deeply ridged area of dirt that had been worn down by walkers exploring the area. Above the boulder, the foliage was intensely dense and thick, and they struggled to orientate around the boulder to find the creek again. Even the sound of the waterfall was absent. On retracing their steps, they realised they had trekked too far away from the original trail. Their relaxing swim and their composure now gone, they were disoriented. And were unsure which direction they had come from.

As they tried to find their way back to the creek, they had moved further and further inland and the bush was getting thicker and thicker. The undergrowth was dense and prickly bushes stung their legs and arms. They struggled to walk. Jann realised then that they were in the thickly forested area beyond the hut. An area she had been first warned was too dangerous to explore. 'We're lost,' Jann said.

'What do we do now?'

Their comfort and, yes, their survival depended on the choices they made from here on. They might have been lost, but they were both fit and carrying plenty of water, having filled up their water bottles before leaving the swimming hole. And they still had some bread, cheese and a couple of apples in their backpacks.

'Unfortunately, we didn't tell anyone what we were doing today. We hadn't planned on climbing a steep embankment to check the other side of that bloody monster of a geological formation.'

Kat was always calm and steady in her manner, but now showed she was fearful of our situation.

Jann tried to reassure her by saying, 'Don't panic. It's not helpful. We need to plan wisely.'

Jann and Kat were losing daylight and they seemed to be deep in a wilderness area, so they made a decision to find somewhere to spend the night. They ate what remained of their picnic lunch and huddled together for warmth on a bed of ferns that they had scavenged.

The only shelter was the overhang of towering gums. Misty rain had started dripping droplets from the leaves above them. They didn't sleep and neither did the forest animals. So many noises. But they distinctly heard the sound of a gun blast as night settled in. 'That rifle shot came from the direction above us,' Jann said. Whoever it was, or whatever it was, they could not have found their way out of this bush in the dark. They began to fully understand how dire their predicament was.

Darkness enveloped them.

'Will we get out of this?' Kat's body was tense. She grabbed hold of her backpack and placed it under her head.

Jann couldn't settle. Adrenaline still held its grip. So many unknowns. *Will we get through the night unscathed?* Lying on the hard bed of brittle stemmed ferns was a strain on her already fatigued muscles. She felt responsible for the predicament they were in. *I've made too many mistakes?* she thought, as she shifted closer to Kat for warmth. Jann took a deep breath and the familiar smell of moist eucalypt leaves gave her some comfort. 'Of course, we will, Kat.'

'You're right. I'm just feeling spooked.' Kat's tone had softened. She sat up and touched Jann's arm. 'Do you feel abandoned by Tom?'

Her question took Jann by surprise. But Kat was always first to ask the key question. 'I did at first, during those first few days after Tom left. But I don't feel that way now.'

'What do you mean?'

'I must admit that this year hasn't been easy. I often felt vulnerable, but mostly I felt disappointed.'

'Disappointed in marriage?'

'No. Not disappointed in marriage. Disappointed that, for years, I pretended we were doing okay when, in fact, we weren't. I regret that I didn't have the courage or the insight to recognise what was happening to us. We unwittingly conspired together for years, each of us lost in secrets and imaginings.' Jann paused, then asked, 'What about you, Kat? You've had your share of disappointments.'

Kat moved. Her breath was warm on Jann's face. 'I was disappointed when my husband left for a younger version of me. And now? Well, how do I reconcile the love I have for someone who is married to the church?'

Kat's comment hung heavily between them and Jann felt some strange comfort in a shared story.

We've both been hurt, Jann grieved. *And now we are both lost in this bloody bush.* But she kept her thoughts to herself.

Dawn. It was mild. They sat together in silence. The increasing light showed the forest was still thick and dense around them. Their damp clothes clung to them as a reminder of their plight. Any embarrassment about their morning toilet had long since gone. Jann was determined to find the fire trail on the escarpment above their property. She had walked it many times before. She now felt confident in her determination to get them both home.

The sound of water nearby alerted them to a clearing in the underbrush. The forest fell away and they came face to face with the creek.

'The creek was nearby all the time. We were seriously disoriented, weren't we?' Kat said.

'Yes. But we made the right decision to stop before nightfall.'

'Yes. And we are no longer lost,' they almost yelled in unison, in the crisp morning air.

'Which way now?' Kat asked.

Jann pointed downhill. 'Look! That's Knuckles' place with

the smoking chimney and further down beyond that you can just about see my hut and home.'

It was Knuckles' rifle shot that had rung out across the bush to give them a sense of direction to walk to safety. How did he know they hadn't returned from their creek walk? How did he know they had planned to walk in the creek? She would never know the answer. And Knuckles wouldn't tell her, either. 'He must have seen us at some time as we started on our walk,' Jann told Kat. His presence in Jann's life would always remain a mystery. In her year in the bush on her own, Jann was beginning to understand that she was never really alone.

Swollen knees, scratched calf muscles and an exhaustion she'd never known greeted her as she arrived back at the hut. Several cups of brewed tea later, with a pillow propped under her knees, she felt it was the most comforting, restorative brew she'd ever had.

Leaving It All Behind

The removalists were due to arrive early. The truck would stop inside the main gate. All Jann's furniture and boxed possessions would have to be brought to the truck. The removalists had said the dirt track to the creek's crossing had, 'Too many potholes and was far too narrow for safe passage.' Besides, once loaded, they could not guarantee a safe return to the front gate without getting stuck.

Jann's decision to leave the property was an easy one. Her connection to the place and the community she had become close to would always remain a significant part of her life story. She had realised that to stay would be to live out a lifestyle goal that had been intended as a shared journey, not for her alone. The property needed the two of them, she always knew that. Everything about the land required daily physical effort. Managing the hut's energy supply, maintaining the vegetable garden, keeping the thistles down, looking after the fruit trees, keeping the kangaroos and wombats out of harm's way, collecting and chopping wood for the combustion stove, driving long distances for work, for supplies and for social outings. The hut was comfortable, but it was also restrictive — the bathroom was a cupboard-sized space with no toilet. But it was the isolation as well as the challenges she had faced during her time alone that helped her to make the decision to return to their house in the city.

When Jann had returned from a trip to Central Australia, she found some neighbours' cattle had broken into her vegetable garden, trampled and eaten the lot. They had been rounded up and herded safely back into the neighbouring paddock. An apology and assistance to repair the damage had been given. She stood in front of the wire netting with a gaping hole and surveyed the trampled mess. She saw the folly of all the effort needed to make repairs and the work required to plant more vegetables, and her decision to leave was confirmed.

Packing up her belongings took several weeks. Jann and Tom had stored the bulk of their furniture and effects in the large shed behind the old cottage. Three years previously, they had done a thorough job of storing their excess furniture on a raised platform and covering the area with a large tarpaulin as a protection from dust and rats. Except the flea-bitten wombat had dug and made a home underneath the raised area. The removalist had organised and delivered flattened cardboard boxes to the front gate, which she had collected and carted across the creek bed to the hut.

How to begin packing up her life on the farm? It wasn't possible to pack up the three years Jann had invested building on her married life in this new landscape. It wasn't possible to pack up twenty years of accumulated memories by putting them away in a cardboard box. 'I'm living on a knife edge,' he had shouted at her, before he left that final weekend. That memory would never be able to be packed away and stored until needed again. It would hang around as the ultimate dismissal, cutting through her. 'You can have the lot,' he said, as he departed.

Jann felt physically drained. She remembered reading a popular garden presenter's advice when confronted with a neglected garden: 'Just one square metre at a time. That's all it takes — small steps.' Strong, clear advice if you're not dealing with the emotional toll of reconciling her family stuff. 'That is now my family stuff,' she mused.

She started packing her books. Something concrete to remember the person she was at the time she read them. So many copies of books read with notes folded and found between the weathered pages. Amongst them she found Scott Peck's *The Road Less Travelled*. She flipped through some of the earmarked pages and remembered his sage advice on solving relationship problems. Even while his personal life was in turmoil — infidelities and finally divorce. The book's title makes reference to one of Robert Frost's poems, another writer she admired. She and her husband had taken a risk by choosing the road less travelled by resigning from their conventional jobs to live in a rural community. They could not see very far down that track at all. Why hadn't Jann read the signs and made the decision to stay in her comfortable home with her adult children close by?

She picked up Orwell's *1984*. A study text for senior students. It was a challenge to teach literacy appreciation to uninterested teenagers, the children of forestry workers. She had wanted to use more contemporary texts like the works of Germaine Greer, Anne Summers or Marian Sawer. 'I don't think so, Jann,' the school Principal had advised. 'What might be good for the ACT goose would not do for the bush-area gander,' he had said. And had smiled at her naivety.

Some years later Jann would discover that such material would not be acceptable to the taste of the Queensland gander, either. Understanding a community that depended on logging for their livelihood was an important lesson for her. After school on her first day, she had been rewarded with a full-length scratch on her car. 'Get rid of that conservation sticker,' the principal had said. Jann soon learnt to utilise students' interests as a springboard in her lesson planning. However, her TAFE position teaching adults to communicate well in their capacity as volunteers had been a stabilising term of work for her, coming as it did on the back of their separation. Her teaching resources were neatly organised and boxed together.

She looked through some family photos. 'I'm absent,' she said out loud. 'Invisible. I'm not absent. I took most of the bloody photos capturing the children's birthday parties, picnics at the swimming hole, bushwalking, camping, our family on holiday in Tasmania.' The photos were now a source of sadness, but the images in her head were not. Her favourite photo was from a family trip to a national park. The four of them with arms locked around each other and walking in a line. Our family together. It made her tearful to look at it now.

Her pottery teapot — a gift from Tom for her thirtieth

birthday. It had sentimental value because it represented years of comfort in routine. Loose leaf tea, freshly brewed twice a day. A ritual that brought them together each morning and afternoon. Time to chat about plans for the day, time to be together. Wrapping the pot, she placed it carefully aside. 'To travel with me,' she noted aloud, 'not to be packed in a removalist box.'

Their much-loved furniture. Particularly their oval dining table with bandy Queen Anne legs that had been at the centre of the family's life since the children were little. The table had been discovered in the backyard of a friend's house and was in a state of disrepair. Tom had recognised its value and worked on it over many weeks to bring it back to its former glory. The family had read together on the table, they had each studied for their degrees on the table, they had celebrated birthdays, eaten dinner together.

Jann couldn't stop reliving the past. Time to get on with reality. She anticipated the memories would be a lot harder to deal with when she unpacked the lot in her once familiar surroundings on her return to the house in the city.

She boxed up loose items in the hut. The bulky furniture was loaded onto a neighbour's trailer and driven to the front gate in readiness for the removalist. Similarly, all the furniture from the shed was brought down to the front gate. She had made a trip back to the city with a car load of loose items, plus two cats.

The evening before Jann was to leave, she sat on the edge of the verandah at the front of the hut and looked out beyond the creek and beyond Knuckles' place to the distant hills. She felt the enormity of all that she'd had to do to pack up and leave. She had given notice of her return to her long-term tenants in the city.

She had resigned from her teaching position. She had farewelled her colleagues, students and friends. Tears started to form as she thought about the unknown in front of her. She started to sob then, heaving sobs of unexpressed grief. Her body felt wracked with the grief of too many years. Hold on. Just keep holding on. Everything will be okay. At times, she felt like a failure; her dreams lost. They never really talked to each other about Tom's infidelities and what was really behind his actions. While she had been hurt and could not see past the infidelities, she now understood that, perhaps all along, he was trying to find himself and meaning in his own life. And in the end, they didn't know how to break up well. He had written many years later that, in a very deep way, his marriage to her 'was not freely entered into' by him.

Relationships go through lots of changes and challenges. Getting married, having children, studying, starting a job, moving house. All built on a foundation of hope. Although loving someone can be uncertain and plain agonising at times, hope kept her searching for a happy ending. But it was never going to be okay. Jann had hoped they would grow old together and her sadness was that it would never happen. They had been too young, and doing the 'right thing' had forced them to conform to the mores that society expected of them.

In her years of teaching, Jann had experienced the power of the 'raging hormones' of youth. She was so glad that things had changed and that the young now had freedom to live and, above all, freedom to love or at least to make love.

One last walk. Jann followed the tyre tracks and strolled towards the river crossing; a slow walk noticing vividly the bush around her. The kiwifruit vines, one male, one female on the gable end of the hut, now starting to fruit. The track worn so deeply from so many car trips, the pumpkin patch growing out of control, amassing weeds and grasses, the fenced garden with her trampled precious herbs amongst dislodged rocks, the ditch where she had dug and shovelled dirt for the hut, now becoming overgrown. Tree trunks fallen on the creek bed after the windstorm, dislocating stepping stones at the creek's edge. The sound of the creek behaving normally after the flood. She returned to the front of the hut across her freshly mowed grass.

Her last night in the hut. Her last night in the bush. 'I'm leaving all of this behind. I'm leaving something behind to be passed on for others to build on.' Or so she told herself. That part felt right.

Jann slept on her yoga mat on the earth floor. The hut was empty of furniture. The mud walls were pitted and cracked in places now; exposed when she removed the furniture. She opened the window overlooking the garden that was partially blocked by the blooming lemon tree. She breathed deeply as she drank a single glass of fresh tank water. A few remaining dishes was all she needed for her breakfast of bread and cheese. She left the single empty glass and placed it on the ledge in front of the window overlooking the vegetable garden. For the new occupant. Just in case.

One last look around. The door to the hut firmly closed. Jann didn't look back. The track to the crossing, the rocky creek, the pitted dirt road to the front gate. Stopped. One last time. She wound down the window and put her arm out and waved in a gesture of farewell. Leaving it all behind.

*

Now, thirty years later, she walked back the length of the track to the main gate and, as she looked back towards Mount Tantawangalo, she was reminded of lines from a poem in Robert Frost's book *Mountain Interval* that was titled 'The Road Not Taken'.

She and Tom had been on a road less travelled in modern times. On the road of a past era. Each in their own way had been attracted to the ideals of a pioneering life. They had not taken the well-trodden path to embrace the comforts of city living. And neither had they wanted to be hemmed in by the conventions of city life. Such are the dreams and hopes and yearnings of youth.

*

Yes, it had been an 'interval' but never a sojourn. She knew now that she had learned so much about life and relationships, and about hard work, and how she had grown with the experience from her time on the property.

She started the car and the car radio blared a song from the local station: 'Non, je ne regrette rien!' The defiant tones of Edith Piaf and *No Regrets* filled the air. 'Good on you, "Little Sparrow",' Jann shouted. She roared the lyrics in unison as she headed to her home in the city.

END

References

The following are some of the works used in researching this story:

Callaghan, Edith Joan, *Memories of Wild Duck,* unpublished, 2006.

Dowling, Collette, *The Cinderella Complex*, Summit Books, New York, 1981.

Frost, Lucy (compiled by), *No Place for a Nervous Lady: Voices from the Australian Bush,* McPhee Gribble/Penguin Books, Melbourne, 1984.

Frost, Robert, *Selected Poems of Robert Frost*, with an Introduction by Robert Graves, Rinehart Edition, New York, 1963.

Goethe, Johann Wolfgang von, *On Commitment,* LiveJournal, online source, 2022.

Greer, Germaine, *The Female Eunuch,* MacGibbon & Kee, London, 1970.

Peck, M. Scott, *The Road Less Travelled,* Rider, USA, 2012.

Summers, Anne, *Damned Whores and God's Police: The Colonization of Women in Australia*, Penguin Books, Melbourne, 1975.

www.ingramcontent.com/pod-product-compliance
Lightning Source LLC
Chambersburg PA
CBHW030302010526
44107CB00053B/1788